Becca M. Wander

"Can I Fire the Fu€%£r?"
A guide to the employment dismissal process in the UK

ISBN 978-1-716-29914-8

Copyright © Becca M. Wander 2022

The right of Becca M. Wander to be identified as the author of this work has been asserted in accordance with the Copyright, Designs and Patents Act 1988.

All rights reserved. No part of this publication can be reproduced, stored in a retrieval system, or transmitted, in any form, or by any means (electronic, mechanical, photocopying, recording or otherwise) without the prior written permission of the author.

This book is sold subject to the condition that it shall not, by way of trade or otherwise, be lent, hired out, or otherwise circulated without the author's consent in any form of binding or cover other than that which it is published and without a similar condition including this condition being imposed on the subsequent purchaser.

"The secret of change is to focus all your energy not on fighting the old but on building the new."
Socrates, Greek Philosopher

"Can I Fire the Fu€%£r?"
A guide to the employment dismissal process in the UK

Contents	Page
Introduction	4
Picking a target	5
Choosing your weapon	8
Loading the gun	13
Taking aim	16
Looking down the barrel	20
Pulling the Trigger	23
Fire!!	25
Checking the Target's been hit	29
The Inquest	31
About the Author	34

"Can I Fire the Fu€%£r?"
A guide to the employment dismissal process in the UK

"Dealing with employee issues can be difficult, but not dealing with them can be worse."
Paul Foster, CEO and Founder of The Business Therapist

Introduction

Did you hear the one about the clown who was sacked from the circus? He claimed Funfair Dismissal! Now, that's the only joke you'll hear in this book but there may be some lighter moments as this is a serious tome written for the lay person, the man in the street, for those who employ and are employed. It's short, sweet, and simple – like my wife!

And there's the problem, right there. You can't use phrases like that in the workplace in case you offend someone. You can't say someone's short as they could be suffering from a disability that restricted their growth.

And if you're a man, you can't say someone's 'sweet' as it could be sexist. Why is that sexist? Well, would you tell another man they were sweet? If you say something to one sex that you would not say to another, then it's likely to be sexist!

And simple? That's a no, no. Telling someone they're simple could imply they suffer from a mental health condition that impairs their ability to learn.

It outlines the process for fairly dismissing an employee under UK law and plays on the word 'firing' when discussing a dismissal. It is written for the employer as well the employee because the law applies equally to both parties. So, whether you're a Cowboy or an Indian, take note of your rights and responsibilities.

Now, you get an idea of how this book is written - think of Lord Sugar in a cowboy hat – the commercial world is like the Wild West, there's plenty of Cowboys out there, some Sheriffs, many Indians, and plenty of bullets to dodge!

Although it is written in a (hopefully) light-hearted fashion it is as factually correct at the time of writing but, in the spirit of 'serious' law books, please seek independent legal advice before dismissing someone or where your dismissal is being considered.

Best wishes and enjoy!

Becca M Wander

Picking a target

"It doesn't make sense to hire smart people and tell them what to do; we hire smart people so they can tell us what to do."
Steve Jobs, Business Magnate.

People don't start a business thinking about HR issues and how they'll manage them, and they don't hire people thinking one day they will need to fire them.

Perhaps this chapter should be entitled, *'Who's put themselves in the firing line?'* because there are circumstances when an individual may be at risk of being fired (or dismissed) through no fault of their own - on the ground of redundancy, for example.

But I'm getting ahead of myself, so let's start with the basics.

There are (currently) five fair reasons to dismiss an employee but before we even look at those we need to decide if someone is an employee. This is the most important aspect in this book because only if someone is employed, do we need to look at dismissing them and decide whether such a dismissal will be considered to be fair.

Who decides whether the dismissal will be fair? An Employment Tribunal because they are the ones who will decide if your actions accord with the law and, if not, what amount of compensation should be awarded to the individual as a result of your actions. And this point is critical, the Employment Tribunal doesn't decide on a case by asking itself, *'would we have dismissed this employee in these circumstances?'* Instead, it must ask itself, *'did this dismissal fall within the 'band of reasonable responses' available to the employer?'* If it decides that a reasonable employer would have dismissed in these circumstances, it will be a fair dismissal.

However, if the individual is not an employee, no dismissal will arise and therefore who cares if the dismissal was fair or not – other than the individual who's now out of work – as they would not be able to submit a claim to an Employment Tribunal.

Similarly, even if the individual is employed, you can still dismiss that person without reading or following another word in this book, just be warned you will not succeed in defending your actions at an Employment Tribunal, you will lose the case and you will be penalised in terms of the amount of the award made to the individual for your failure to follow a correct procedure.

If you are that assassin (and a rich one who is not concerned about following a legal process nor about paying individuals for your failings) then read no more, you've wasted money on this book (although you've made me very happy!).

The law defines an employee as someone *'employed under a contract of employment.'* That seems straightforward but what if the employee wasn't given a contact of employment, or they have failed or refused to sign it, are they still an employee? Of course they are, probably.

In the absence of a written contract of employment the law will consider what basic employment rights they have under statute. The main statute dealing with work-related issues is the Employment Rights Act 1996. In addition, the Working Time Directive covers issues such as holiday entitlement and rest breaks, and the Equality Act 2010 deals with, among other issues, discrimination, harassment, and victimisation.

In the absence of a contract of employment, the law will consider the employment relationship and will determine whether that person is considered to be an employee.

When deciding if someone is an employee an Employment Tribunal will consider what degree of control the company has over that individual when it offers them work. In its basic form, if the company does have control over the individual the law equates this to a 'master and servant' role whereby the master tells the servant what to do, how to do it, when to do it, where to do it, and so on. In this scenario the servant is employed by the master.

Taking an opposite example, if I have a leaking tap and I call a plumber to fix the problem, they'll tell me when they will arrive at my premises, they will consider the problem, use their own tools to fix the leak, and will provide me with an invoice for payment.

The plumber is free to do the job himself or to ask a colleague, apprentice, or trainee to do the work and I have no say in the matter. Although they have undertaken work for me, I haven't employed them because the above elements of control are missing from the relationship. They've told me what they will do and when they'll do it, not the other way round and, on that basis, they are truly self-employed and no employment relationship exists.

This differs from an employment relationship whereby the company will tell the individual what work to do, when to do it, how to do it, where to do it, and the company will usually provide the necessary tools to do the job – which may be a desk, chair, pen, computer, hammer, scalpel, etc.

In some business sectors, such as garage mechanics or engineering works, an individual may use their own tools, but this will not negate an employment relationship as the company will still have control over the work and how, when, and where it will be undertaken.

In certain circumstances the employee will tell the company what, when, and how work needs to be done, but this doesn't stop that situation from being an employment relationship.

Consider someone who is disabled, perhaps confined to a wheelchair or bed-ridden and requires constant or daily care. They may employ someone or several people to provide for their needs and even though those individuals will be responsible for providing care to that individual, they can decide when and what work is needed. However, they will still be an employee.

The company may decide to utilise staff via an agency whereby the company informs the agency what they require, and it will offer staff to the company on an ongoing or fixed-term basis. In this situation, even though the company will tell those individuals what work needs to be undertaken, when it needs to be done, and the company may provide the necessary tools required for the job, they will not be employed by the company. Why not?

The reason is because the individual supplied by the agency can decide whether or not to accept the work. They may, in certain circumstances, provide someone else to do the work for them. Even though they provide their services to the company, their contract is with the agency who offers work to them. In effect, the individual is being loaned to the company for a fee.

Nevertheless, it should be noted that under the Agency Workers Regulations 2010 those individuals are entitled to be treated in broadly similar terms as staff employed by the company during their tenure. They have the right to be treated on a par with the company's staff in terms of equality.

On that basis, the company is not the employer, the company doesn't have to offer them work if the company no longer want them the business. They simply tell the agency the individual is no longer required and their work for the company ends at that time.

In addition, there is the scenario that falls between these examples such as circumstances where individuals are employed for a specific task (construction building, for example) for a specific period of time or for the conclusion of that project. These individuals are usually engaged under a contract **for** services (as opposed to the above contract **of** service in an employment relationship) and are classed as a worker, rather than an employee. Workers also have specific rights, one of which is the right not to be unfairly dismissed.

However, let us assume our individual is an employee, we need to decide how we want to end the employment relationship in a manner that won't result in the company losing money as a result of that firing.

What we cannot prevent is the individual submitting a claim to an Employment Tribunal for unfair dismissal. But we can, if the steps outlined in this book are followed, reduce their chances of success, and remove any allegation of procedural unfairness.

So let's look at the reasons that entitle you to fairly fire an employee.

Choosing your weapon

"How do you fire an employee with a bad attitude? The right way."
The Grocery Store Guy

As discussed in the previous chapter, only someone employed by the business can bring a claim against the company for unfair dismissal. If they are unable to bring a claim, the company won't suffer any financial penalties, or detriment in terms of adverse publicity.

Furthermore, in order to bring such a claim the individual is required to have been employed by the company for a period of not less than two full years. Of course, there are exceptions to this rule which we will deal with later but, as a starting point, if the company is considering firing someone for something they have done (or not done), the employee must have the necessary length of service to be able to submit a claim to an Employment Tribunal.

Now, I'm not suggesting the company act in a cavalier manner with any individual who has less than two years' service but, if the employee has been employed for less than two years, you could fire them for any spurious reason. If you don't like their new haircut, shoes, tie, handbag, or any reason that is not due to anything discriminatory, there will be no Tribunal come-back.

Having said that, it is my strong recommendation that the company should - no, must - treat all employees the same when it comes to matters of dismissal and you should disregard their length of service to ensure a correct and fair procedure is followed. The company should get into a habit of correctly following their procedures with all staff regardless of how long they have been employed.

Turning to the Employment Rights Act 1996, it states there are five fair reasons to dismiss an employee. They are on the grounds of:
1) conduct (or to put it correctly, misconduct),
2) capability (or lack of ability),
3) redundancy,
4) legality (or illegality) and, where the previous reasons don't apply,
5) for some other substantial reason.

Some of these reasons may appear obvious but we will look at each reason for a greater understanding of their meaning as, in law, some words have a different meaning to those used in everyday language.

Section 94 of the Employment Rights Act 1996 states, *'an employee has the right not to be unfairly dismissed by his employer'* (for 'his' also read 'her') and section 98 states the principal reason for the decision to fire someone should be for one of the reasons stated above. Let's look at these reasons in more detail.

Conduct
When we consider someone's conduct it's usually them doing something they're not supposed to have done, or them not doing something they have been asked to undertake.

Depending upon the circumstances it may be justifiable for that person to lose their job. Theft is one example whereby it would be fair to fire someone. However, you must be satisfied (in terms of having supportive evidence) that the person has done what they are alleged to have done, but more on that later.

Capability
Whereas with conduct there is an implication that someone has purposely done something they should not have done, or purposely not done something they should have done, capability indicates they are not able to do the particular thing required of them, no matter how much training, support, or guidance they are given.

It strikes at the heart of their ability to perform their duties. An extreme example being someone who cannot perform brain surgery as they were employed as a cleaner.

Now I'm sure a company wouldn't usually expect or ask someone employed as a cleaner to undertake brain surgery but if that person was unable to adequately clean the premises for which they were employed, would their dismissal for that reason be considered to be fair?

If they had been given adequate training, the necessary tools to do the job, had been supported by their employer when they asked for help, had been given sufficient guidance in what they had failed to do, they had been told what they must do, and had been given time to improve but no improvement had materialised, then the dismissal is likely to be fair.

Redundancy

Section 139 of the Employment Rights Act defines a redundancy situation, and when a dismissal on such grounds may be fair. It requires a particular process to be followed which, if not followed correctly, could turn a fair dismissal into a procedurally unfair dismissal which will be reflected in the award of damages granted to the successful claimant.

In short, a redundancy situation arises:
　i.　when there is no work for a particular employee to do, or
　ii.　where the business needs less people who all do the same job, due to a reduction in the volume of that work, or
　iii.　due to the business closing, or
　iv.　due to the business closing and relocating somewhere else.

Whereas the above are definitions of a redundancy, the company will be required to show there is a genuine redundancy situation. It must then meet and consult with the affected staff (not necessarily all staff) or their trade union representatives, or in the absence of a trade union, employee representatives elected by the staff. The length of time it will take to conclude the process will depend upon the number of staff the company is considering dismissing.

If the number of redundancies is likely to be between 20 and 99 staff within a 90-day period, consultation must last at least 30 days before the first dismissal for redundancy is made; for 100 or more staff the consultation period must not be less than 45 days.

There is no timescale for redundancies up to 19 staff and the period of consultation can be significantly reduced, which may benefit a company in financial difficulties.

The consultation meeting is intended to inform affected staff of the reasons leading to the company's decision to make redundancies, and for those staff to put forward any thoughts, ideas, suggestions, or proposals that would avoid the need to make them redundant or would reduce the numbers required to be made redundant.

The company should consider all such proposals and provide reasons if those suggestions do not alter the company's position. As such, several meetings may be required to discuss and explore each proposal.

Any failure on the company's part to consider such proposals could lead to allegations that the business is 'just going through the motions' or it is a 'tick-box' exercise and is not meaningful. Such failure may result in a finding of unfair dismissal.

It may be alleged the redundancy was only designed to reduce the wage bill and, perhaps, be more attractive to a potential purchaser of the business, for example. It is therefore imperative that a business can show justifiable reasons for the redundancy and that there is no other option available to it. As a rule of thumb, the company must show that by taking this action the business will benefit, and by not taking this action the company will suffer.

Once the consultation period has ended, in the absence of any plausible suggestions being made or alternative work being available, the affected staff should be notified they are dismissed on the ground of redundancy. They should be informed of their entitlement to a redundancy payment, if they have the necessary length of service. Again, two years' service with the amount calculated on their weekly pay, number of years employed, and their age.

If alternative work is available (and suitable to them), the employee is entitled to a trial period of up to four weeks to decide whether or not they wish to continue in the alternative role without losing their entitlement to a redundancy payment. Alternatively, an employee who refuses an offer of suitable alternative work may forfeit their entitlement to a redundancy payment.

In some cases, and as appalling as it may sound, the Covid-19 pandemic justified some businesses in reducing their workforce unnecessarily whereby staff were told they were redundant due to a downturn in work which may only have been temporary. Some businesses then employed staff on revised contracts and reduced salary, taking advantage of the economic climate and knowing those staff need to work for two years or more before they acquire employment rights.

Whereas I make no judgement on those businesses, at best they are stretching the law to their own benefit and are probably themselves morally redundant (and like I say, I make no judgement on them).

Legality
I've referred to this as legality but the Act refers to someone being unable to perform their duties because of an enactment preventing them from doing so.

In layman's language, and by way of an example, if someone employed as a driver loses their license on conviction of a driving offence resulting in them being unable to drive, dismissing them may well be justified as they are unable to perform the duties for which they were employed under their contract of employment.

Some Other Substantial Reason
This is the catch-all reason that doesn't fall within the above categories.

Using the example of our cleaner above, due to reasons unconnected with that person's ability to clean, let's say they have a child who attends school with a child of a manager at the client premises they clean and those children have an argument resulting in the client's child being expelled.

Let's say the client complains to the Managing Director who states they no longer want your employee on their premises. Is it fair for you to dismiss the cleaner in these circumstances?

If that client business is your only client and you cannot offer the employee any work of any kind, then you could fairly fire them even though they have done nothing wrong, or certainly nothing that could be considered to be misconduct. Indeed, they could be a model employee attending work on time and doing an excellent job. There are no capability issues, they aren't redundant as their role still exists, and there's nothing preventing them from attending and undertaking their job. But if they have been refused access by your client, for whatever reason, they could be fairly dismissed on the grounds of 'some other substantial reason' through no fault of their own.

Having considered the five fair reasons to dismiss an employee, what might be an unfair reason to fire someone?

What if the employee crossed the road without looking and caused an accident, would it be fair to fire them? Probably not, unless they are employed as a lollipop person. But what if they were employed as a road construction worker and they had been told by their manager to cross the road to get a particular tool, would their firing be fair?

The employee could argue they were acting under instruction and that work could not continue until the tool had been acquired, would it be fair to fire them for that?

What if the accident resulted in a vehicle crashing into fencing owned by the company thereby resulting in damage to their property? What if it were fencing owned by a neighbour and it caused damage to their property, would that make any difference to the fairness of the firing? What if the vehicles that collided had resulted in the death of one or more persons, would that make the firing of that employee fair?

Maybe, but the point is, it depends on the circumstances and the incident will need to be investigated and a meeting held with all relevant parties in order to determine the full facts before any decision is made and we consider these points in the next section.

Loading the gun

"The way to get started is to quit talking and begin doing."
Walt Disney, Entrepreneur.

What evidence is needed to reach a decision that could lead to the fair firing of an employee?

Well, following an allegation being made against someone, the matter will need to be thoroughly investigated. Depending on the findings, the individual must be offered the opportunity to answer the allegation(s) against them at a disciplinary hearing prior to a decision being made. The decision must be based upon the evidence available at the time of the disciplinary, including the individual's responses to the allegations.

In circumstances where criminal proceedings are being brought against an individual, it is a misnomer that a disciplinary hearing should be put to one side pending the conclusion of the police investigation. The police have a higher burden of proof when dealing with criminal matters – being sure of the individual's guilt (previously, beyond reasonable doubt) – whereas in civil matters the burden is only on the balance of probabilities – is it *more likely than not* that the individual was at fault.

In all circumstances, the company should appoint an Investigation Officer to investigate the circumstances. In the example in the previous section, this may involve checking any CCTV footage of the incident, speaking to the driver of the vehicle to determine their version of events, determine if there is an in-car camera showing the incident, contacting any witnesses who saw what happened, and speaking to the employee to obtain their version of the events.

That all seems straightforward and sensible. However, what if the driver left the scene of the accident and cannot be traced? What if no camera footage exists or no-one was around to witness the incident? What if the employee says the driver appeared to be driving erratically and they simply ran across the road to avoid being hit by the car?

In short, you have only the individual's

version of the events and you're left with damage to the company's property caused by the vehicle. This is where the balance of probabilities kicks in and the Investigating Officer needs to decide what version of events they prefer.

They may want to consider such questions as:
- Is it more likely than not, that the driver of the vehicle was driving so erratically that the employee feared for their safety and believed that running across the road was the safest option?
- Is it more likely than not, that that the car would have crashed into the fencing if the employee was not present?
- Why would the driver decide to leave the scene of the accident?
- Did the employee obtain the details of the car and the driver?
- Why would the employee lie about the events?
- What does the employee have to gain or lose by lying?

These are all pertinent things to ask and the only person available to answer such questions is the employee. Their replies will determine whether any action is taken against them and whether it should proceed to a disciplinary hearing.

What if they had told a colleague earlier in the day that they were going to meet a friend who owed them money, and the friend drove the same make and model of vehicle the employee stated had caused the accident? Would that impact on the outcome of the investigation?

What if the other side of the fencing contained expensive tools or materials that could be sold without trace for a considerable sum? Was the vehicle driver intending to steal the tools? This could explain why the driver didn't stop after the incident.

Did the employee innocently discover the attempted theft, or did they know the driver and tipped them off about the materials causing them to leave the scene when they saw someone in the road?

Either the employee was involved in a traumatic incident in which they were scared for their safety, or they have lied about the circumstances. The Investigating Officer will need to decide, on the balance of probabilities, which version of events they believe to be correct.

Clearly this is a difficult decision and one that could result in serious repercussions for the employee and the company, which may never discover the actual true account of the incident. The Investigating Officer can only act on what they genuinely believe to be the true version of events.

What if, in a different scenario, an employee is seen by a manager taking money from the company's till and putting it in his pocket; the incident is caught on CCTV, and the employee denies the allegation, should they be fired?

It all seems clear-cut; the employee was doing something they weren't meant to be doing and was attempting to steal money from the company.

However, the same process outlined above needs to be followed - investigate the matter and give the employee the opportunity to explain their actions in a formal disciplinary hearing.

Let us suppose that, after their initial denial of stealing the money, the employee was suspended from their duties and invited to attend an investigation meeting. During the meeting they stated they were owed the money because a previous customer required change and there wasn't enough money in the till so they paid them from their own pocket. They explain they were merely taking what was due to them. Sometimes the investigation needs to consider all situations and all likely possibilities.

Based upon the employee's explanation the CCTV footage may well support their assertion. If the till had been checked, it may show a deficit in funds which would support the employee's claim.

The point here is to act quickly and appropriately to determine the true facts without making any immediate assumptions regarding what may have happened.

At the conclusion of the investigation, having spoken with the employee and anyone else who may be able to assist the Investigating Officer in reaching a decision, when all available evidence has been gathered and considered, the outcome can be provided in writing to the employee. That decision will either be no further action is taken against them or they are invited to attend a disciplinary hearing to answer allegations the Investigating Officer considers to be relevant.

We'll assume there is sufficient evidence to proceed to a disciplinary hearing and we will look at how to conduct such hearings in the next section.

Taking aim

"Your choices reflect your hopes, not your fears."
Nelson Mandela, former President of South Africa.

The person holding the disciplinary hearing, the Disciplinary Hearing Officer, should not, where possible, have been involved in the matter previously - such as witnessing the events or by investigating the issues. On that basis the Hearing Officer can claim they are an impartial person.

Nevertheless, they are also an employee of the company, they are accountable to their line-manager, and will always be open to allegations of bias or undue influence, whether actual or perceived. For those reasons it would be better to arrange for an independent third-party to hold the disciplinary hearing to avoid such assertions, but more on that later.

Also, it should also be noted that I've mentioned the Disciplinary Hearing Officer will be accountable to their line-manager. If the Managing Director or Owner of the business was to conduct the disciplinary hearing it may scupper the individual's ability to appeal (if they have grounds to do so) or to have a fair Appeal Hearing.

For the Appeal Hearing Officer to avoid allegations of coercion they will need to be of sufficient status that they can overturn the decision of the Hearing Officer without fear of retribution. They may not want to change a decision if they have to account to the Managing Director who was the Disciplinary Hearing Officer. In short, keep the Managing Director free to hold any subsequent appeal hearing following the outcome to the disciplinary hearing.

It is always best to try and deal with the issue in a manner that would avoid a subsequent appeal. That could only be achieved by investigating the matter thoroughly and, depending on the findings, hold a disciplinary hearing and reach an impartial decision based upon the available evidence.

When holding a disciplinary hearing, the Hearing Officer should keep an open mind regarding the circumstances until all the evidence has been provided to them and the employee has had an opportunity to relate their version of events and provide responses to questions.

To act to the contrary will leave the Disciplinary Hearing Officer open to allegations by the employee that they did not listen to their responses, that the outcome was a foregone conclusion, or that the allegations were designed to remove them from the business.

This could be countered by asking the employee why the company would want to remove them from the business, why would the company benefit from the individual's removal, and why would the company invest so much time and resources in dealing with this matter if they simply wanted to fire the employee? If no reason can be given by the employee for such assertions, and if the Hearing Officer listens (and listens intently) to the employee's replies, they can avoid such accusations.

At this stage we need to consider the seriousness of the allegation and whether it falls into what is known as a 'gross' misconduct issue.

There are degrees of misconduct, from the perceived low-level failing to contact the company when an employee is off sick from work for example, to the more serious rudeness to colleagues or customers, to gross misconduct involving theft, attending work under the influence of drink or drugs, fighting in work, or intentional damage to company property.

The sanction for someone found to have committed an act of gross misconduct is sometimes referred to as 'summary dismissal,' which means the immediate termination of their employment with no entitlement to notice pay.

The purpose of deciding the level of misconduct is to determine the likely sanction. If the issue is likely to fall within gross misconduct you might want to consider suspending the employee pending the outcome of the process. I can already hear the chants from employment lawyers and trade union representatives screaming that suspension is no longer a neutral act by an employer but a pre-determined decision likely to cause irreparable damage to the employment relationship if that employee was subsequently not sanctioned with dismissal and was invited to return to work.

In my view, the first question put to you by an Employment Tribunal would be why, if you considered the matter to be so serious that it was likely to lead to the dismissal of the individual for gross misconduct, did you allow them to remain in work until the conclusion of the process?

It should be noted that suspension of an employee is on full pay, so they suffer no financial loss. If they are exonerated, or given a sanction less than dismissal, their return to work can be managed to avoid any adverse actions by colleagues or detriment to the individual. If this is borne in mind from the outset, suspension can still be considered as a neutral act, pending the outcome of a fair process.

Now, having invited the employee to the disciplinary hearing it must be noted they do have the right to attend with either a work colleague or, if they are a member of a trade union, a trade union representative.

What if, following the invitation in writing to the employee to attend the disciplinary hearing, you are informed the representative is unable to attend? Section 10 of the Employment Relations Act 1999 states a postponement of no longer than five working days can be granted, either to enable the representative to attend, or for the employee to obtain alternative representation.

It should be noted that the right of representation does not extend to a particular trade union representative. In other words, if the chosen representative cannot attend at a particular time and the employee requests a postponement, they can be asked to enquire if an alternative representative is available at the proposed time of the disciplinary hearing.

Having obtained the employee's acceptance of the disciplinary hearing date and time, it is now for the employee to answer the allegations and challenge or dispute the evidence and put forward their version of the events. The allegations against the employee will have been notified to them in the letter of invite to the hearing and it will have enclosed all documentary evidence upon which the Hearing Officer will rely when conducting the hearing.

The disciplinary hearing should be held in a private setting where the conversation cannot be overheard and it won't be interrupted by telephone calls, visitors, colleagues, or the general public. The hearing should be confidential – what is said in the hearing should stay in the hearing.

In order to allow for the hearing to flow, you should consider having a note-taker present to record what was said, what questions were asked, and what responses were made to ensure a comprehensive written record is taken of the discussion.

In the absence of a note-taker (or in addition to) obtain the employee's agreement for the meeting to be audio-recorded whereby a verbatim record can be obtained by transcribing the recording to have an accurate account of what was said and by whom. This will avoid any confusion about what was discussed and it may help any subsequent appeal if any party alleges they didn't make a particular response or comment.

Following the introduction of all persons present at the disciplinary hearing, put each allegation to the employee, show them the evidence that has been provided to you, any relevant witness statements, and invite them to respond to the allegations one by one.

Instead of challenging the employee's responses (which may be perceived as being confrontational), question the reason for them acting in the manner alleged, or failing to act in an appropriate manner. Allow the employee the opportunity to respond to the allegations and allow them to ask any questions, present their evidence and call any witnesses. Their companion or representative should be asked if they have any questions they want to ask.

The disciplinary hearing should not be threatening in any way but it should be conducted as courteously as possible, allowing the employee to speak freely. Try not to become embroiled in an argument and do not make any disparaging or humiliating remarks. Remain calm and do not raise your voice or make any physical gestures that could be interpreted as threatening.

Use open questions to ensure you understand the circumstances of the incident, and closed questions to confirm what the employee has said to you. The purpose of the disciplinary hearing is to establish the facts so a fair decision can be reached regarding the allegations.

During the hearing the representative is entitled to sum-up the employee's case but not to answer questions on their behalf. It's worth repeating, *not to answer questions on behalf of the employee*, as the employee must be the one to answer the allegations.

When the employee has provided a response to the allegations, the evidence has been considered, and any witnesses questioned regarding their involvement, check if the employee or their companion has anything else they wish to say. This will ensure the employee has had every opportunity to say what they want to say and that they have been treated fairly and reasonably during the process.

Once all responses have been exhausted and the employee and companion have confirmed they have nothing else they wish to add, the meeting can then be brought to a close. Inform the employee when they can expect an outcome to the matter in writing.

At this stage it should be noted that evidence will fall within either hearsay (when someone alleges they were told something by somebody else), documentary evidence (paperwork), witness evidence from someone who states they saw what happened, and electronic evidence such as CCTV.

Different weight should be given to particular evidence. CCTV may show what happened and could be more reliable than witness evidence. Documentary evidence is more likely to be more accurate than hearsay evidence, although that doesn't mean the content of the hearsay evidence is wrong, it just may not be as reliable as other forms of evidence.

Only following the conclusion of the disciplinary hearing when the employee has been given every opportunity to respond to the allegations, they have said all that they wish to say, when all the evidence has been shown to the employee to which they have responded, and all further enquiries and investigations have been undertaken by the Disciplinary Hearing Officer, can a decision be reached.

If the disciplinary allegations are upheld, the employee should be informed of the company's sanction against them and these are discussed in the following sections.

Looking down the barrel

"Good decisions come from experience. Experience comes from making bad decisions."
Mark Twain, Author.

Let's pause for a moment. Before a decision is reached and provided to the employee let's consider some 'what ifs'.

- What if this individual has been a problem to the company who want to remove them from the business?
- What if the business is in financial difficulty and could benefit from reducing its wage bill?
- What if the company believes the employee did what they are accused of doing but it doesn't have the necessary evidence to support a finding of gross misconduct?
- What if the Managing Director simply wants this person out of the business because they are concerned about some form of adverse publicity regarding the matter?

There is a process that can be implemented at any time with any employee which is called a Settlement Agreement. It is not a firing of that individual nor a resignation on their part, but a mutual (well, from the company's side anyway) ending of the employment relationship.

As the name indicates, it is a formal agreement that must contain specific elements for it to be binding on both parties. The main purpose though is for the company to pay the employee an amount of money for them to agree to leave the business. In return, the employee agrees to waive their rights to submit a claim against the company to an Employment Tribunal for their failure to follow a correct dismissal procedure. It can be quick, easy, and less expensive than firing someone via the normal channels.

The difficulty is, deciding how much to offer an employee in these circumstances. I've found that the most successful negotiation under this process comes from the timing of raising the prospect of a Settlement Agreement as, usually, the business wants to pay the individual the least amount of money it can get away with, but the individual wants to maximise the amount they receive.

There are many reasons why a company would want to make such an offer to an employee, regardless of those listed above. For example, there may well be a genuine redundancy situation but the company prefers not to follow the procedure and may well offer the employee an amount of money, as an incentive, in addition to what that employee would receive if they were to be made redundant. The company might include an enhanced reference, over and above a standard one, to assist the employee in obtaining future employment, which could be persuasive in getting the employee to accept the offer.

I can already hear screams of "inducement" from employment lawyers and trade union representatives but hang on, in order for such Agreements to be binding, the employee needs to obtain independent legal advice from authorised providers (usually a solicitor or barrister) who can advise the individual whether or not to accept the offer.

I've taken some leeway here because, at this stage, the employee has already agreed to accept the company's offer and until all parties (the employee, the legal advisor, and the company) have signed the Agreement, it is not binding and either party can walk away until all signatures are obtained.

In terms of negotiating a Settlement Agreement the algorithm is simply how much the company is willing to pay in order for the individual to leave their employment, compared to what the employee is likely to accept in order to put themselves out of work.

Be aware though, many mortgage protection companies won't pay out in this situation as they view it as the individual volunteering for unemployment. Similarly, the Government views it in the same light and the individual won't have recourse to Universal Credit for a specified period of time. Clearly, if an individual can walk straight into another role (and the enhanced reference may assist) the Agreement may seem like a windfall for which they will willingly accept.

If agreement is reached the formal Settlement Agreement needs to be drafted and provided to the employee detailing the amount offered in settlement (which must also state their contractual entitlements such as notice pay in accordance with their contract of employment and any accrued but untaken annual leave) and when it will be paid.

The contractual entitlements will be subject to statutory deductions of income tax and national insurance contributions so it is best to state the amount the individual will receive in their hand after deductions have been applied to avoid any misunderstanding at a later time.

There is currently an option to pay an employee an amount free of tax (excluding their contractual entitlements) up to £30,000.00 (not that many Agreements reach anywhere near this figure), but it is an additional incentive for the employee to accept the offer.

Having provided the Agreement to the employee they must then obtain independent legal advice for which there is an expectation the company will provide a contribution (usually the full cost) for the employee taking such advice. This ensures the Settlement Agreement is binding as it avoids any allegation of strong-arming by the company in having the employee sign the Agreement. It also protects the company as the employee cannot later claim they did not understand, or know of the implications on them, of signing the Settlement Agreement.

To ensure compliance, the legal advisor is also required to sign the Settlement Agreement to confirm the individual was given such advice. The company will then sign the Agreement whereupon it then becomes binding and, providing the individual receives the agreed payment in the agreed time, the matter is concluded.

If this is the outcome to the matter, the gun can be lowered as no firing will be made and the employment relationship ends on the date specified in the Settlement Agreement.

For now, let's assume no Settlement Agreement is made or reached and the dismissal process continues.

Pulling the trigger

"Firing people is one of the worst parts of running a company. Actually, in my own experience, I think it's the worst."
Sam Altman, Entrepreneur

Following the conclusion of the disciplinary hearing the Disciplinary Hearing Officer should inform the employee a decision will be made within a specified time. If it is likely to take longer than originally anticipated because of the volume of information for example, or because further enquiries need to be made, keep the individual updated on its progress.

The employee will want to know the outcome as soon as possible but it is better to ensure a correct decision is made rather than a quick one. This will avoid allegations that the Disciplinary Hearing Officer didn't listen to the employee, or they didn't consider the evidence, or that it supports the employee's assertion the company wanted to remove them from the business.

Take time to consider the issues, don't make any snap decisions, investigate and speak to any witnesses or anyone you believe could assist in making a fair and reasoned decision regarding the allegations. It is possible you may need to reconvene the disciplinary hearing if additional evidence comes to light following these investigations as this should be put to the employee so they can offer a response.

Having considered all the issues, when the evidence has been studied, when any additional information has been obtained and put to the employee, and when the responses by the employee have been considered, the Disciplinary Hearing Officer needs to reach an informed decision. The decision should not be influenced by any external factors or by any individual as, should the company have to justify the finding to an Employment Tribunal Judge on oath, it could lead to a finding of Unfair Dismissal.

When a decision has been reached, set out in writing the allegations and detail the responses provided to you by the employee. Outline what investigations you undertook and refer to any documentation provided to you and/or information supplied to you by witnesses. Refer to the evidence and/or witness statements and give your decision to each allegation. Detail your findings and provide the employee with the decision in writing stating whether the allegations are upheld or not.

The outcome letter to the employee should state what, if any, sanction will be given to them, when it will commence, and for what period it will remain on file. When deciding upon a sanction consider the following,
- what sanction has been given to other employees in similar circumstances,
- the employee's disciplinary record and whether it includes any current warnings,
- their length of service, experience, position in the company,
- any mitigating circumstances which could adjust the severity of the sanction,
- whether the proposed sanction is reasonable when taking account of the circumstances,

- if any training, coaching, or support may be required to avoid such circumstances arising in future.

The following is a list of likely outcomes and sanctions following the conclusion of the disciplinary meeting:
- No further action to be taken – when the allegations are not upheld.
- A letter of improvement – for minor misconduct or unsatisfactory performance issues.
- A verbal warning – issued in writing for less serious misconduct issues.
- A written warning – for serious or repeated misconduct issues.
- A final written warning – for more serious or repeated misconduct issues.
- Dismissal with notice – for serious and repeated misconduct issues.
- Dismissal without notice – for issues deemed to be gross misconduct.

We will consider these in the next section.

Fire!!

"The day firing becomes easy is the day to fire yourself."
Tom Peters, Author.

Having discovered the incident, investigated the circumstances, held a disciplinary hearing, listened to what the employee had to say and considered the evidence, it's now time to decide what to do.

Not all outcomes will result in the firing of an employee, it may be that the Disciplinary Hearing Officer accepts the explanations offered by the individual and decides to take no further action against them. On that basis, the matter ends there.

The Disciplinary Hearing Officer may decide to accept some points, but not others, and decide to impose a sanction less than dismissal. Ordinarily, a company will have an Employee Handbook which will contain suggested sanctions for specific incidents of misconduct and these may fall within a verbal warning (which, contrary to its name, should be notified to the employee in writing), a written warning and, if a written warning has been issued previously, a final written warning which gives the employee one last chance to mend their ways otherwise the next step is dismissal.

A verbal warning is usually issued for a period of 6 months and, if no further conduct issues arise (not just the same conduct issue that led to the issue of the verbal warning but *any* misconduct), the matter will conclude. If there is a repetition of the issues the above process will start again. If no further misconduct occurs for the duration of the warning, it is expunged from the individual's file and they start afresh with no warnings.

A written or final written warning is usually kept on file for a period of 12 months before being removed, providing no further misconduct issues arise. In fairness to the employee, no warnings should be issued for a period longer than 12 months as it would be hoped that this period would be sufficient for them to improve their conduct and keep it to a standard expected by the company. Any longer and it could be perceived as being overly harsh to the employee.

The outcome should also take into consideration whether such issues have arisen previously by other employees and what sanction was given to that individual. Be mindful that such decisions set a precedent so, if a similar incident has happened before by a different person and the individual was given a verbal warning, if you were to issue a written warning this time the employee could appeal stating the decision in this instance was too harsh because their colleague was previously given a lesser sanction.

If a written warning was previously given to another individual in similar circumstances but you feel a verbal warning is more appropriate this time due to notable differences, it is unlikely there will be any come-back by this employee. Nevertheless, be aware if it occurs a third time by another individual you could be bound to issue the lower sanction unless you can explain why you haven't followed the previous precedent.

The issue of such sanctions (which must be confidential but you can't stop colleagues talking to one another) should prevent similar actions being committed in future. If you become aware that staff are doing similar things you might want to inform the whole workforce they must stop doing that particular action.

If the employee is as difficult or as problematic as the company believes and it wants them removed from the business, issuing a sanction less than dismissal may give the individual the opportunity to turn into a model employee. This isn't a criticism as the employee may have seen the error of their ways and be thankful they have been given an opportunity to remain in employment.

Alternatively, they may continue to act in a manner entitling the company to invite them into a further disciplinary hearing following which they may be dismissed on the totting-up procedure (verbal, written, and final written warnings being previously issued to the individual), and the company could argue it gave them several opportunities to improve which they failed to take.

However, if the allegation against the individual is for a gross misconduct issue and is upheld, they can be fired, dismissed, shown the door, booted out.

The final decision, whatever the outcome, should be provided to the employee in writing. This doesn't mean they can't be informed in-person or by telephone but, in any event, the decision should be confirmed in writing. They should also be given an opportunity to appeal the decision within a reasonable (for both parties) period of time.

It should be borne in mind that despite the decision to terminate someone's employment, they may have been a hard-working and loyal employee up to the point the incident arose so there's no need to be disrespectful to that individual, afterall they are losing their job, income, status, respect, and this may not be the last you hear from them.

There's no need to hit them between the eyes but the letter should state the reasons for your decision as well as the evidence that was relied upon when making your decision. This is crucial because, should you end up in an Employment Tribunal, they will want to know what information you had before you when you made your decision.

It may well be that further information comes to light at a later date that exonerates the individual, but that is immaterial if you weren't aware of it at the time you made the decision to dismiss. Even if the decision to fire this employee was shown to be based on inaccurate information leading to an unfair decision, an Employment Tribunal may well still rule in the company's favour if you can show you relied on particular information you believed to be accurate when the decision to fire was made.

As stated, the outcome letter should state the individual has the right to appeal the decision to terminate their employment. This isn't just a second go by the employee for someone else to consider the information and see if they reach a different decision, but it must provide information that would entitle someone else looking at the matter with a fresh pair of eyes the opportunity to overturn the decision to fire.

Under the (now former) employee's contract of employment, if they are dismissed with notice – in other words, for a reason that is not gross misconduct - they will be entitled to a period of notice, usually one week for each full year of employment up to a maximum of 12 weeks. This means they could remain in your employment until they have completed their notice period. This may be useful if they need to hand-over work to their colleagues, or complete a particular project, or return any company belongings in their possession.

It also has the downside of them potentially causing disruption within the workplace, which I will leave to you to consider such possibilities.

If their contract of employment allows, they could be paid in lieu of them working their notice so they leave immediately and will receive their notice pay plus any other contractual entitlements – such as accrued but untaken holiday, commission, bonus payments, etc.

In the absence of such a clause in their contract, or if they had access to sensitive information for example, you could put them on 'garden leave' for the period of their notice. This means they sit at home (or in the garden) on full pay and doing no work until the notice period expires and it gives you time to make any necessary changes in work without them being present.

If they are fired for a gross misconduct offence, they leave work immediately, they don't pass Go, they lose their entitlement to notice pay, and are paid only to the date they are fired.

Just consider that point for a moment. If someone is dismissed for gross misconduct, they must have done something so serious that it goes to the root of the employment relationship which means you cannot, CANNOT, allow them to remain in work. The implications of that on the individual are immense.

If and when the employee applies for another job they will be asked the reason for them leaving their previous employment. They could bluff the reason but if the prospective employer asks you for a reference, well, it's unlikely that individual is going to be employed by anyone in the near future so it will affect that person's work prospects for a long, long time.

The point is, dismissal for gross misconduct is rare but you should have no doubt the person did what is alleged before you decide to fire on this ground.

Checking the target's been hit – or, re-loading the gun

"Firing someone is much worse than hiring someone."
Mark Goulston, Business Consultant.

As mentioned, the (now former) employee has the right to appeal the outcome to the disciplinary hearing. The appeal is not just another opportunity for the employee to have a second go at exonerating themselves by having someone else listen to their responses and consider the evidence. Their grounds of appeal should contain some information that wasn't available to the Disciplinary Hearing Officer at the time they made their decision (with an explanation as to why it was not available), or state that the Disciplinary Hearing Officer overlooked or did not consider some vital piece of information.

Both of these grounds should explain why, had the information been available to the Disciplinary Hearing Officer, it is likely they would have reached a different decision. Alternatively, the employee should show that the decision was perverse whereby all the evidence points to and supports a particular finding, but the outcome was the opposite of that evidence.

If the grounds of appeal merely state the individual wants to exercise their right to appeal the decision, they should be asked to explain their grounds for doing so and what further information they have, if any, that would alter the outcome. This shouldn't be seen as being obstructive or refusing to follow a proper process but, unless there is something provided by the individual that would cast doubt on the original decision, it is unlikely to change the outcome and would be a waste of everyone's time.

That said, if and when the individual does provide more comprehensive reasons for appealing, an Appeal Hearing should be convened to listen to their argument. Failure to do so could result in accusations being made that the company refused to follow its or ACAS's process, which could also strengthen the individual's argument that the company wanted rid of them, or the process was not impartial or that the outcome was a foregone conclusion.

Similarly, by following the appeal procedure on what may be perceived to be futile grounds, it will show the individual, an Employment Tribunal, and your staff that you take such matters seriously, that you abide by your obligations and procedures, and that you are a fair and reasonable employer.

In accordance with a fair process, the appeal hearing should be convened by someone not previously involved in the matter.

A process similar to the disciplinary hearing should be followed whereby the individual should be offered the right to be accompanied by a colleague or trade union representative, the hearing should be confidential, a note-taker and/or audio-recording should be taken, and the Appeal Hearing Officer should allow the individual to state and explain each ground of their appeal and why it would alter the original decision.

This is the employee's opportunity to detail why the decision to fire them was wrong. It will also give the company some insight of the individual's argument should the matter end up in front of an Employment Tribunal Judge.

At the conclusion of the appeal hearing the individual should be informed when a decision will be made and the Appeal Hearing Officer should consider all points presented to them, make any further enquiries, and reach a decision based upon that information.

If no additional evidence is produced by the employee, it is unlikely the Appeal Hearing Officer will have any grounds to overturn the original decision, unless they accept the decision was perverse.

If there are grounds to overturn the decision, the individual should be allowed to return to work, be paid any lost salary, and continue as if the dismissal did not occur. It may well be that some form of sanction is made against the employee but that shouldn't stop them from returning to work and carrying on as normal, no matter how difficult they may perceive this to be.

Whatever the decision, the individual should be notified in writing of the Appeal Hearing Officer's decision, advised how the decision was reached, informed that this ends the disciplinary process, and told that the matter is now concluded.

The Inquest

"I didn't see it then but it turned out that getting fired from Apple was the best thing that could have ever happened to me."
Steve Jobs, Business Magnate.

The above process should be the end of the matter but, in the unfortunate situation the individual submits a claim to an Employment Tribunal – for which they cannot be prevented from doing, it is (presently) a free service so it is at no cost to them – here's a few things to bear in mind.

The initial stage of the Employment Tribunal process requires the individual to contact ACAS and advise them they are considering submitting a claim. ACAS will then contact the company to see if there's any room for settlement to avoid that individual from proceeding with their claim.

Don't dismiss this initial contact by ACAS as the Tribunal process can be burdensome in terms of preparation time, attendance by possibly several of your staff (the Investigating, Disciplinary Hearing, and Appeal Hearing Officers for a start), and the cost of representation at the Hearing - unless you want to do this yourself.

In an Employment Tribunal each party bears their own costs and it may be commercially beneficial to pay the individual a nominal sum (less than it would cost you to defend the matter) regardless of the moral consideration. You won't need to re-employ the individual, they may just want a better reference and some money to assist them in the short-term so don't approach any negotiation in an emotional manner but a commercial, protection-of-your-business approach. If settlement is reached in this manner the matter is put to bed and it goes no further.

If no settlement is reached and the individual submits a claim for unfair dismissal in the Employment Tribunal (for which they have three months to do so) you will receive a copy of their complaint and you get your opportunity to respond to the claim. Unfortunately, you have only 28 days to provide your response and be advised this is a strict deadline, responses have been struck-out for being submitted within seconds after the deadline date.

Your response to the claim is an opportunity to state why you believe the decision to dismiss was the correct one in all the circumstances. Also, the claim will be phrased from the individual's perspective and they may have omitted some crucial points within their claim which will allow you to state the full details of the incident and process leading to their firing.

Whereas the individual will receive a copy of your response, the Tribunal will not throw out the claim just because they believe you have a better argument, it will still progress to a full hearing irrespective of each side's standpoint.

However, arguments can be included in the response that if it is found the individual had no prospect of succeeding with their claim (in effect, wasting the Tribunal's time with a futile submission) you can apply for your costs in defending the matter to be paid by the individual. This has the effect of telling the individual you're up for the fight so they better have a good case because if they don't, they may have to stump up the cost of your representative, which may be several thousand pounds.

I can again hear hordes of employment lawyers and trade union representatives shouting about the unfairness of this, but it weeds out the nonsense claims submitted by individuals in the hope they can make a few quid from their former employer, despite the fact they may have previously committed heinous acts which led them to being fired, just saying.

Despite the above, if the matter progresses to an Employment Tribunal hearing the company will be asked, in great detail, the reason for firing the individual and what evidence the Hearing Officer had before them when they reached their outcome.

The Employment Tribunal will consider whether it was reasonable for *the company* to have made that decision. I've italicised this because it is not, and I repeat NOT, whether the Tribunal would have dismissed this individual in these circumstances but whether a reasonable employer (you, if you've followed a correct procedure by looking at the evidence, held a disciplinary hearing, listened to the individual, considered all the evidence in an impartial manner, and correctly dealt with any appeal) would have dismissed in the same circumstances.

If so, you're home and dry. If not, you'll have to pay the individual an award of damages (compensation) based upon their losses (of salary if they haven't secured alternative employment - they will be asked what efforts they've made to find alternative work) as well as a basic award calculated in the same manner as a statutory redundancy calculation.

Whereas the media reports huge figures being awarded to individuals, according to the Ministry of Justice, the average award for unfair dismissal in the year to 31 March 2020 was £10,812.00. This figure was £9,801.00 for dismissals due to race discrimination, £17,420.00 for sex discrimination, and £27,043.00 for disability discrimination.

Awards for discrimination are unlimited and are based upon what the Employment Tribunal believes would be equitable (quite high if they want to punish you).

Don't let this latter point worry you, just follow the guidance laid down in this book, by ACAS, your internal procedures and processes in your Employee Handbook, and impartially considered the evidence in your possession when reaching the decision to fire someone. Easy really.

About the Author

"Business is about making others' lives better"
Richard Branson, Entrepreneur

I've always been curious about the statutory rights of employees and what action can be taken if those rights are breached. In the 1980's employees would strike if they felt aggrieved by their employer (the one who pays their salary and enables them to have a mortgage, pay bills, clothe their children) but what about those individuals who aren't in a trade union or who cannot afford to strike, what do they do if the employer isn't doing what they've been told they would?

In 1996 the Government enacted the Employment Rights Act which put into black and white the rights of employees, the obligations on employers, and strengthened the liability on employers for not complying with the law.

Over the next couple of decades the law in this area has evolved and expanded and we now have a raft of laws, case law, ACAS guidance, and social media. This latter point is mentioned simply because disgruntled ex-employees can cause harm to a business that don't follow their own procedures. They can become an ex-employee if they post unfavourable (and untrue) things about their employer (the one who pays their salary and enables them to have a mortgage, pay bills, clothe their children) on social media platforms.

This book is intended to assist employers in doing what they are meant to do as a reasonable employer. It's not targeted at the large national companies (although the law applies to anyone who engages the services of someone else) but at the smaller companies who may not have an HR function and may be uncertain regarding what action they should and can take against an employee who acts in a manner that may be harmful or detrimental to the company or their colleagues.

It is not intended (in any way, shape, or form) to be a statement of the law, but an outline of the actions an employer needs to consider before taking disciplinary action against someone in their employment. Please, please, please take advice from a professional before dismissing an employee to avoid a successful claim of Unfair Dismissal being brought against the business. If nothing else, follow the procedure outlined in the above chapters and make all decisions on a commercial basis rather than an emotional one.

It was reported by ACAS in May 2021 that the cost of resolving workplace conflict was £1,141 for each disciplinary matter based upon 6 days management time. If you want to save time and money, and if you don't want to take the above action, contact me at **HR Onsite** on enquiries@hr-onsite.com at www.hr-onsite.com and I'll hold the meeting for you.

At HR Onsite we say we are the future of HR. This is because, in my 25 years' experience in advising and representing companies at Employment Tribunals, the process and procedures are becoming more legalistic. By outsourcing investigation meetings, disciplinary, grievance, capability, and appeal hearings, redundancy consultation meetings, return-to-work interviews, or by holding mediation sessions, you can show to an Employment Tribunal that you took the employee's concerns seriously, that you didn't want to just get rid of them as alleged, that you engaged the services of a professional company to consider both sides' arguments, who recommended an outcome based upon the available evidence, and produced an independent and impartial report detailing the above for the company to consider.

This benefits the company and the employee and shows to your staff you are a fair and reasonable employer, regardless of what they may say behind your back!

www.ingramcontent.com/pod-product-compliance
Lightning Source LLC
Chambersburg PA
CBHW041545220526
45473CB00014B/2964